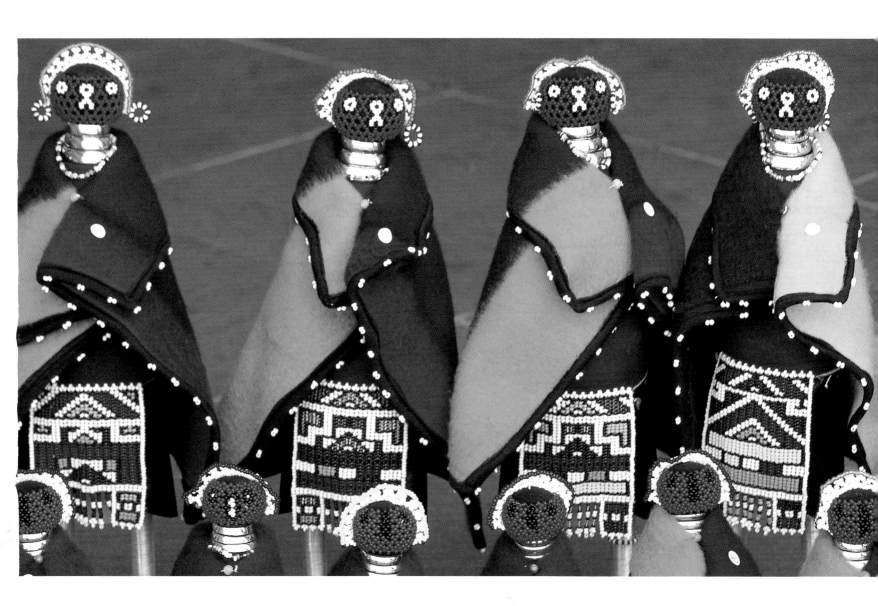

SOUTH AFRICA

SEAN FRASER

CONTENTS

11

INTRODUCTION

South Africa is undoubtedly the gem in Africa's crown and, as the continent's most significant tourist destination, it enjoys a worldwide reputation for its scenic splendour, the diversity of its many peoples and their wide-ranging cultural influences. South Africa is not simply a country of open veld and endless sky, smiling faces and a fascinating heritage: it goes far beyond these simplistic notions. It is Africa's newest democracy, a symbol of victory and an icon of hard-won freedom for the world at large.

The warmth of the nation as a whole is echoed in the abundance of its land, the limitless horizons and vast open spaces that have come to epitomise this small part of Africa. There are times when one can scarcely take it all in, such is the beauty of this land. The people of South Africa have, over the centuries, suffered great pain and been faced with enormous challenges, but have emerged with a spirit undaunted by deprivation and oppression. Shining from this country is a brave, new outlook, and a fierce determination to succeed.

PAGE 1 Beaded Ndebele dolls

PAGES 2–3 Zebras

PAGES 4–5 A baobab tree

PREVIOUS PAGES A windmill pump in the Karoo

OPPOSITE Namaqualand daisies

OVERLEAF Blaauwklippen estate in the Western Cape Winelands

PAGES 14–15 Boys at Still Bay, on the southern Cape coast

THE CAPE
PENINSULA

Endowed with extraordinary natural beauty and a sophisticated urban atmosphere, the Cape Peninsula is the gateway to southern Africa, and the country's top travel destination. It boasts a remarkable selection of popular tourist attractions and counts as its drawcards a number of natural landmarks that make the Mother City one of the greenest and most attractive on the continent. Dominating the city is the Table Mountain National Park, encompassing the famed mountain, Kirstenbosch National Botanical Garden, the Cape of Good Hope and Cape Point.

THE VICTORIA & ALFRED WATERFRONT

Life in Cape Town essentially centres around the City Bowl and the picturesque harbour at its foot. **Table Bay** (PREVIOUS PAGES) is part of the Atlantic Ocean that extends beyond the eastern seaboard and surrounds the Peninsula. It was on these wave-lapped shores that indigenous peoples like the Khoi gathered sustenance from the sea and where the first Europeans settled in southern Africa. It is here – against the magnificent backdrop of mountain and sea – that Cape Town still entertains its citizens and visitors, some of whom arrive on **luxury cruise liners** (LEFT). What started life in the colonial era as a simple victual-ling station, and slowly grew into an all-important stop on the trade routes to the East, is now an up-market tourist destination. The **V&A Waterfront** (ABOVE) is South Africa's most significant drawcard, one that stands proud among similar developments in the USA and Australasia. Combining the historic architecture of a bygone era with the most up-to-date facilities and services aimed at an ever-demanding public, the Waterfront is today the premier stopover for shoppers, visitors, sightseers and an endless parade of locals.

Robben Island

Just eleven kilometres offshore lies that icon of hard-won freedom, the indomitable **Robben Island** (RIGHT). Having seen service as a prison, a hospital, a leper colony, a military base and a nesting ground for seabirds, the island is now preserved for posterity lest the world forget the pain and hardship experienced by those banished to its god-forsaken isolation. It was here, in **Cell No. 5** (ABOVE LEFT), that the island's most famous political prisoner, Nelson Mandela, wrote his biography during the 18 years that he spent on the Island. He spent the last eight years of his imprisonment in Pollsmoor and Victor Verster prisons. He was released in 1990 and went on to become the first President of a truly democratic South Africa.

Today the Island is a haven for a variety of wildlife, including the African penguin and steenbok. As a World Heritage Site, the Island is strictly monitored to ensure that development is restricted and that there is little or no impact on its landscape.

THE CITY BOWL

Guarded by the big grey bulk that is Table Mountain, the City Bowl is the very heart of Cape Town, the beating pulse of its lively people, with its busy streets and its endless stream of traffic. Although Cape Town's **central business district** (PREVIOUS PAGES) remains every inch that of a modern, contemporary First World city, with an intricate network of **highways and thoroughfares** (ABOVE LEFT), much of its historic architecture is a legacy of either the Dutch or British settlers, who bequeathed to the nation the remarkable examples of traditional Cape Dutch façades and rows of filigreed Edwardian and Victorian townhouses – such as those of **Long Street** (ABOVE RIGHT) – that now lie interspersed with towering skyscrapers and plush new developments such as the inspiring **Arabella Sheraton** and **Cape Town International Convention Centre** (OPPOSITE). And yet, despite the heritage of the colonists, Cape Town retains the flavour of a truly African urban metropolis. Its roads, side streets and pedestrian malls such as **St George's Mall** (ABOVE CENTRE) are inevitably dotted with a plethora of street vendors and market stalls.

Cape Town – People & Places

As the Mother City and one of the country's most prosperous centres, Cape Town is home to an extraordinary diversity of people, who together add the colour – both literally and figuratively – to the modern city. Today, many Cape families can trace their lines back to the early Khoi inhabitants, the Dutch and British colonists and the hundreds of slaves indentured here in the days of the fledgling colony, and the many Nguni-speaking peoples who made their way to the Cape, and who brought to it their indigenous culture, most notably, their languages and traditional lifestyles, including their **arts and crafts** (ABOVE CENTRE). Of the many different contributions made by various members of local communities over the ages, one of the most significant must be of those descended from the Indonesian and Malaysian slaves and prisoners brought here by the Dutch settlers. Even today, in the very heart of the central urban area, the historic **Bo-Kaap** (OVERLEAF) – where so many of these individuals and their descendants were settled – remains the quintessential mix of old and new that has come to epitomise modern Cape Town.

Table Mountain & Environs

As one of the world's most significant biodiversity hotspots, Table Mountain is the showcase for one of the country's World Heritage Sites – the Cape Floral Kingdom which blankets its steep slopes. It is also the centrepiece of the Table Mountain National Park, which covers the entire Peninsula and extends from the mountain's highest reaches, all along its spiny ridge to the windswept coastline of Cape Point and the Cape of Good Hope.

Embraced by the pinnacle of Devil's Peak to the east and the hooded bulk of Lion's Head to the west, the remarkable biological riches of Table Mountain – from the feathery leaves of its fynbos vegetation to its numerous small mammals, such as porcupine and rock hyraxes (known locally as dassies) – are not only of great significance to the biodiversity of the Peninsula, but also the drawcard that attracts so many visitors to Cape Town. They come to walk its many winding paths, climb its valleys and, from its summit, reached by the famed cablecars of the **Table Mountain Aerial Cableway Company** (RIGHT), to marvel at **the city at its feet** (ABOVE).

THE ATLANTIC SEABOARD

Just below Signal Hill and the **Twelve Apostles** (ABOVE), the rocky ridge that skirts the city's western seaboard, is a string of soft, white-sand beaches that have become synonymous with Cape Town and its laid-back lifestyle. This Mediterranean-style strip, which extends from Three Anchor Bay in the north, along the Atlantic coast, to Llandudno in the south, is hot property – in almost every sense. Protected by its mountain backdrop and a series of rocky outcrops that separate the small bays from each other, this is the idyllic beach destination ever-popular among trendy locals and hordes of visitors. In summer, the icy seawater notwithstanding, the fierce sun beats down on rows of sunbathers and others enjoying the café culture. Virtually all the luxury mountainside homes and beaches here – Sea Point, Bantry Bay, Camps Bay, Bakoven and Sandy Bay – boast unsurpassed sea views. As a result, chic hotels such as **The Bay** in Camps Bay (LEFT) are the perfect play-ground for high-profile international stars who keep homes along this 'African Riviera'.

THE SOUTHERN PENINSULA

Linking the 'sunset strip' of the Atlantic seaboard and Hout Bay to the deep south is a long and winding road that takes in what is probably the most impressive stretch of mountainside and sea views in the entire country – **Chapman's Peak Drive** (PREVIOUS PAGES). This precarious stretch of mountain road offers a unique outlook over the ocean and the waves of the Atlantic as they crash on boulders.

Much further south, beyond the pristine beaches of Chapman's Bay, Noordhoek, Long Beach and Kommetjie, lies one of the Cape's least disturbed and most beautiful conservation areas, the **Cape of Good Hope** section of the Table Mountain National Park, and, at its southernmost tip, the wild and windy **Cape Point** (ABOVE and OPPOSITE). It was here, in the long-gone seafaring days of the colonial era, that many a vessel saw its end, dashed against a merciless coastline by wind and wave. Today the visitors' facilities and viewing deck (ABOVE) look out over the most notorious stretch of the 'Cape of Storms'.

FALSE BAY & SURROUNDS

Stretching in a curve northward from Cape Point on the eastern side of the Peninsula, lies the False Bay coastline, dotted with a number of small villages, parts of which have retained a distinct colonial atmosphere and a decidedly unhurried way of life. Most notable of these small enclaves is **Simon's Town** (ABOVE), once a vital outpost for the British Royal Navy, and still the home base for the South African Navy. Close by is secluded Boulders Beach, tucked away amid rock and hillside and the officially protected home of a colony of **African penguins** (RIGHT). To help conserve the natural environment here, there is a small charge for admission to the beach. The next stop on the curve of False Bay, after the sleepy town of Fish Hoek, is **Kalk Bay** (OVERLEAF), much like Simon's Town in nature but simpler and more rustic. Here, the dominant activity has for years been its all-important fishing industry. The charming little village has a character of its own, the narrow streets and steep mountain slopes peppered with small galleries, pottery studios, arts-and-crafts outlets, antique stores and bistros.

THE SOUTHERN SUBURBS

As the early Cape settlement expanded and spread beyond what are now the city limits, the tiny outposts to the south grew into established suburbs that attracted families hoping to escape the frenetic bustle of city life. Today, these include Wynberg, Claremont, Newlands and Rondebosch, all of which have become mostly quiet and refined 'villages' in their own right – some even developing 'central business districts' of their own. Close to the CBD of Claremont and Newlands, famed home of rugby and cricket, are the extensive botanical gardens of **Kirstenbosch** (LEFT), acknowledged as one of the finest floral reserves in the world. There is an enormous variety of indigenous vegetation here and the rockeries, pools, amphitheatres and tree-lined avenues offer a rare insight into South Africa's natural heritage. Today the upgraded facilities include a well-appointed gift shop and souvenir outlet, an excellent restaurant and a visitors' centre. These impressive services aside, Kirstenbosch is popular with locals and foreign visitors alike for the famed **summer sunset concerts** staged in the picturesque gardens (ABOVE).

THE CONSTANTIA WINELANDS

The vines that make the wines for which the entire Cape region is world famous were originally planted right here on the Cape Peninsula, in the fertile valleys of the Constantia Winelands – as opposed to the far more encompassing **winelands of the Cape hinterland** (OVERLEAF). While the vineyards of outlying areas such as Stellenbosch, Franschhoek and Paarl may enjoy far more prominence on the international scene, it is Constantia and the surrounding hills that lay claim to the fine tradition of viticulture passed down through the generations. Today, centuries-old estates such as Groot Constantia, Klein Constantia and Buitenverwachting produce some of the best wines the Cape has to offer. The relatively high rainfall of the Cape winters and sultry heat of its summers make the **Constantia Valley** (OPPOSITE) ideal wine country, and wine production here and further afield is now a vital industry with a string of offshoots. Most notable of these is the thriving tourism industry that draws visitors here, as well as the many up-market hotels and five-star dining establishments that have become the hallmark of the Cape.

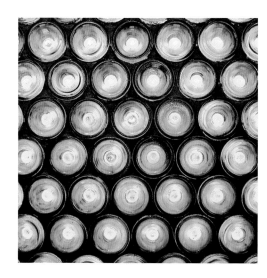

THE CAPE WINELANDS

The rich, fertile soils of the Cape interior make it true wine country, and the seat of South Africa's wine production. The **French Huguenot Monument at Franschhoek** (ABOVE RIGHT) bears testim ony to the viticulturists from Europe who planted their vines here in the 1600s. The towns and villages that sprang up in those early days, such as Stellenbosch and Paarl, remain the heartland of the Cape Winelands. The land and climate of the Cape hinterland offer the perfect conditions for fruit to grow well, and the entire region is now patchworked with orchards and vineyards that add enormously to the area's attraction. The majority of the estates are centuries old and, after being largely neglected over many decades, most have now been conscientiously restored. Many of the most highly regarded estates – including Boschendal, Spier, Nederburg, Simonsig and Lanzerac – boast fine examples of grand old Cape Dutch homesteads. Many estates, among them **Delheim** (OPPOSITE) offer cellar tours, wine tastings and sales, and an abundance of other attractions, including restaurants, museums and a range of cultural activities.

SOUTHERN CAPE
& GARDEN ROUTE

The Southern Cape is an area of great diversity, differing enormously from area to area – from the rugged seascapes of the southernmost point, along the scenically splendid Garden Route to the dry and dusty interior. Whatever the landscape, however, visitors cannot help being impressed by endless stretches of fynbos or snow-white beach sand, densely wooded forest and mile after mile of semi-desert. Perhaps the most inspiring of these vistas is the Garden Route, the expanse of coast on the southern seaboard that stretches from the holiday resort of Mossel Bay to the mouth of the Storms River. This remarkably beautiful countryside extends for about 200 kilometres and all along the route are pretty little towns and hamlets that do justice to the region's name.

THE OVERBERG INTERIOR

While many of the towns of the Overberg, including Robertson, Montagu, Swellendam, Caledon and Bredasdorp, seem to look much alike to the harried traveller, all have a unique feel that adds unmistakeably to their old-world charm. Structures such as the **Dutch Reformed church** in **Napier** (ABOVE LEFT) highlight the sense of community that is increasingly drawing city dwellers. While much of the interior is comparatively dry, parts are remarkably fertile, receiving considerable rainfall. This adds greatly to the productivity of the region, which is renowned for its golden **wheat and canola fields** (ABOVE, CENTRE and RIGHT). In parts, the cultivated countryside gives way to gentle landscapes of fynbos, veld and still waters – one of the finest examples being **Theewaterskloof Dam** (OPPOSITE). The productive farmland may be green and fertile, but the mountains and valleys are rough and craggy and, as you draw near to the Little Karoo, the pastures give way to a dramatically different scene – one of arid plains and dust bowls.

AFRICA'S SOUTHERNMOST POINT

Save for the few areas of human development – fishing villages such as **Kassiesbaai near Arniston** (OPPOSITE) and a few inland, principally farming towns – the Agulhas Plain has largely been untouched for millennia. This is perhaps because of its isolation from the areas of early settlement in the Cape and because the inhospitable terrain here makes life harder than in more fertile parts of the country. It is surprising that this region bears evidence of very early habitation by humans: tidal fishing traps bear witness to the Stone Age peoples that once called this home. The hunter-gatherers who first greeted the 15th-century Portuguese expolorers and the Dutch settlers of the mid-1600s had already long occupied this **rocky coastline** (OVERLEAF) renowned as a 'graveyard of ships', the dazzling white dunes and the scrappy shrubveld further inland. These early inhabitants were also the initiators of what is now an important contributor to the local economy – **fishing**. Many locals still make their living the tried-and-tested way (ABOVE LEFT). The **Agulhas lighthouse** (ABOVE RIGHT), built in the mid-19th century, was modelled on the ancient Egyptian one at Pharos.

OUDTSHOORN & GEORGE

The towns of the Little Karoo that lie in the shadow of the Swartberg and Outeniqua mountain ranges are generally very laid-back. At the heart of the region is Oudtshoorn, once known across the globe for its prized **ostrich feathers** – an industry that, although it no longer rakes in the handsome sums it once did, nevertheless thrives in this rather dry area (OPPOSITE). Here too are the hauntingly beautiful **Cango Caves** (ABOVE LEFT), a natural wonder with a convoluted underground network of tunnels and caverns, once apparently inhabitated by locals who had long since abandoned their grand old dwelling by the time the caves were rediscovered in the late 1700s. Today, environmental controls have been implemented in order to protect the fragile condition of this ancient geological system from the huge numbers of visitors each year.

The capital of the area, George is renowned for its numerous **world-class golf courses** (ABOVE RIGHT), including the acclaimed Fancourt Hotel and Country Club. George and nearby **Mossel Bay** (OVERLEAF) are the gateway to the many treasures of the Garden Route.

KNYSNA

Knysna is the jewel of the Garden Route – a small, even sleepy, town best known perhaps for its oysters, the turacos (commonly referred to as louries) that inhabit South Africa's only true forests and the gentle waters of the Knysna Lagoon. The coastline on which Knysna is situated boasts an extraordinary array of flora and wildlife in a peaceful environment far from the madding crowd. The wonderland of the Knysna National Lake Area is a spectacularly unspoilt expanse that includes the impressive forests, the famed lagoon and the great bulks of the **Knysna Heads** (ABOVE), which guard the fragile ecosystem and wildlife sanctuary embraced within their borders. Within these confines, however, are small, exclusive enclaves – with their breathtaking views and tranquil **lakeside setting** (OVERLEAF) – reserved for human habitation. One of the region's top attractions is a locomotive steam engine, known as the **Outeniqua Choo-Tjoe** (LEFT), which has been in existence for more than a century and continues to cover the rail route between Knysna and George.

NATURE'S VALLEY

The haven that is **Nature's Valley** (RIGHT) is probably the most underestimated on a coast that is blessed with an endless number of charming little getaway spots. For the visitor who makes the effort to soak up its restorative environs and enjoy the splendid isolation it offers, it is a treasure indeed. The area forms part of the heavily wooded Tsitsikamma National Park, which extends along the rugged coast and, as a marine reserve, even into the waters of the Indian Ocean, protecting the creatures that frequent these waters, including whales and dolphins. The adjoining State Forest Reserve, with its giant Outeniqua yellowwoods, harbours an enormous variety of endemic flora (such as lilies and orchids) as well as small mammal species, including grysbok, baboon and duiker. The magnificent **Storms River Gorge** (OVERLEAF) is also part of the Tsitsikamma National Park, and the popular five-day Otter Trail, which takes its name from the rare Cape clawless otter, starts at Storms River Mouth. The **Bloukrantz River bridge** (ABOVE) not only offers scenic views but a boost of adrenalin for those who dare to bungee jump from its towering heights.

EAST COAST &
KWAZULU-NATAL

South Africa's entire east coast – which extends from the northern reaches of the southern Cape, through the Eastern Cape province and up into KwaZulu-Natal – is endowed with a warm, welcoming climate, rich soils and a magnificent coast of crystal waters lined with sparkling beaches. It is indeed the stuff of which travellers' dreams are made. While much of the immediate interior is distinctly rural in character and farming plays a pivotal role in the lives of many of its inhabitants, the coastal strip is dotted with fashionable holiday getaways and, in the case of **Port Elizabeth** (ABOVE), East London and, in particular, Durban, significant urban hubs that drive not only the economies of the region, but also the all-important tourism industry.

THE EASTERN CAPE

The first encounter with the Eastern Cape is defined by the gentle, laid-back lifestyle of its coastal towns and cities and the vast emptiness of its extensive interior. It is a land of shrub and veld, in parts awash with green and a lot more fertile than one might imagine, in others dry and apparently barren. It is here that one finds the showcase of local wildlife – the **Addo Elephant National Park** (PREVIOUS PAGES), home of the region's African elephant and one of the Cape's premier wildlife reserves.

The region's 'green belt' exists in the forests of **Hogsback** (OPPOSITE), and the landscape slowly merges into cultivated farmland and agricultural towns, such as **Bathurst** (ABOVE RIGHT), famed for its giant pineapple, icon of local farming. Most memorable of these is, however, Grahamstown, the town that grew up around the homesteads and farms of the 1820 Settlers and best known today as the seat of some of South Africa's most acclaimed academic institutions. The abundance of churches here has earned it the appellation of 'City of Saints' (ABOVE LEFT and CENTRE).

The Wild Coast

The Eastern Cape's Wild Coast is just that – wild, unpredictable and ruggedly beautiful in its simplicity. The shoreline here is constantly buffeted by wind and sea, evidence of which may be seen in the jagged rocks and uneven coastal plains that extend right up to KwaZulu-Natal. The most famous landmark on this rocky stretch is **Hole-in-the-Wall** (PREVIOUS PAGES), the battered and weathered rock formation that stands as an icon of the broader region. Once part of the apartheid government's 'Bantu homeland' of the Transkei, the region is the traditional home of the Xhosa people who settled here centuries ago and whose cultural influences still leave their mark on the local landscape. Even though the province has seen considerable development in recent years, a large percentage of its people still live a rural lifestyle, and the interior is dotted with **traditional huts** (ABOVE RIGHT), constructed much as they have always been. In the rural areas, the farm-based Xhosa people still practise traditional crafts (ABOVE LEFT) and the customs and rituals, such as **initiation rites** (OPPOSITE), of their forefathers.

DURBAN & SURROUNDS

The city of **Durban** (PREVIOUS PAGES) is one of the country's fastest-growing metropolitan

centres, and is rapidly catching up with the more high-profile Cape Town to become a

showcase for South Africa. Set amid a lush landscape, punctuated with subtropical veg-

etation – including **frangipani** (OPPOSITE) – it was established as Port Natal, the gateway

to the untamed interior of what was then Natalia and an important maritime centre for

the fledgling colony. Today, Durban is not only southern Africa's largest, busiest and

most significant port, but also one of the most popular holiday destinations on the sub-

continent. The extensive seaboard, which runs the length of the entire province, from

Port Edward in the south to Kosi Bay in the north, is a holiday mecca, but it is the string

of beaches and seafront developments on Durban's south and north coasts, for instance

Umhlanga Rocks (ABOVE LEFT) that has become the leisure capital of the entire east coast.

Among its most popular attractions is the oceanarium, the lavish **uShaka Marine World**

(ABOVE RIGHT), a wonderland of marine life and an important research centre.

GREATER ST LUCIA WETLAND PARK

Nestled between the steep slopes of the Drakensberg and the northern shores of the Indian Ocean bordering Mozambique is the Greater St Lucia Wetland Park, 400 square kilometres of coastal forest, lakes, rivers and pristine conservation land that encompasses Lake St Lucia, St Lucia Estuary, the St Lucia Marine Reserve, Mkuze Game Reserve, Cape Vidal and False Bay Park. The waters here and the fragile ecosystems they harbour, probably the most ecologically significant in the entire country, have been proclaimed one of South Africa's World Heritage Sites. The mangrove swamps, network of lakes and **coastal plains** (OPPOSITE) boast not only an extraordinary array of well-preserved **marine fossils** (ABOVE LEFT), but also a bounty of wildlife, including mammals, birds – of which there are hundreds of varieties – and reptiles, from the humble lizard to the **Nile crocodile** (ABOVE CENTRE). Today, although human activity is strictly governed according to rigid environmental controls, the conservation programme includes all-important educational elements as well as **tourist facilities** (ABOVE RIGHT) that help fund the conservation efforts.

Sodwana Bay

Sodwana Bay demarcates the northernmost boundary of the Greater St Lucia Wetland Park (which in turn extends as far south as St Lucia Estuary). The coast – extending from Sodwana north to Kosi Bay, almost on the Mozambique border – boasts waters that are as pristine as you will find anywhere in southern Africa. The underwater world is one of colour and extraordinary life forms, ranging from sharks, stingrays and big-game fish species to clownfish, turtles and a host of marine organisms. Although much of the surrounds comprise wildlife conservation areas and marine reserves, certain concessions (fiercely protected by law) have been made to the tourist market, and the region is perhaps the country's best-known and highly acclaimed angling, deep-sea fishing and diving destination. The marine life here is both colourful and extensive, the corals and fish allowing for some of the most rewarding **diving** (RIGHT) in southern African waters. The area is also well known as the breeding ground for leatherback and **loggerhead turtles** (ABOVE) that make their way to the beaches every year in order to lay their eggs.

Maputaland & Surrounds

Maputaland encompasses the north-eastern parts of KwaZulu-Natal, and its marine resources are considered the most sensitive of the subcontinent, its wildlife congregating around the extensive network of freshwater lakes, streams and rivers, and within the tall grasses and stands of subtropical vegetation that encircle the area. The untainted nature of its environs also means that it continues to draw naturalists, conservationists and tourists keen to experience the pristine conditions of these wilds. The top game-viewing destination is **Mkuzi Game Reserve** (ABOVE) at the foot of the Lebombo Mountains. The great diversity of habitats means that the reserve boasts an equally impressive range of wildlife, from elephant and **hippopotamus**, giraffe and zebra, to terrapin and an abundance of water birds, including flamingo and pelican. The highlight of the northernmost stretch is **Kosi Bay** (OPPOSITE), an intertwining system of winding channels that link a series of lakes. One of the most recognisable features of this watery world are the **fish traps** crafted from reeds by locals who make the most of the wide range of fish in these waters.

THE BATTLEFIELDS

As the 'Last Colonial Outpost', KwaZulu-Natal saw considerable hardship and tribulation during the volatile early years of European settlement – constant skirmishes between the colonials and the traditional communities who saw their ancestral lands taken over by the new settlers. Today, the ruins of the battlefields in the interior of the province bear silent testimony to the bloody wars that raged between Boer and Brit, Boer and Zulu, and Brit and Zulu. The veld where brave warriors once fought and fell and uniformed soldiers defended king and country are powerful reminders of what transpired in those hellish early years, and the monuments that stand here today are all that remain on the sites of such battles as Rorke's Drift, Blood River, Ulundi and **Isandlwana** (ABOVE). This battle-scarred land is also the ancestral home of the Zulu people, a nation gathered together by the legendary chief Shaka in the 1800s. As the royal seat of the Zulu people, the province is still very much the heartland of the nation and the great **warriors** (LEFT) whose forefathers fought here are still held in high esteem.

Mountains of the Dragon

The Drakensberg mountains, encompassing the **Royal Natal National Park** (PREVIOUS PAGES), must surely be South Africa's greatest natural feature, a vast and towering series of **breathtaking peaks** (OVERLEAF), hills and vales that have come to symbolise the pride of KwaZulu-Natal. Extending virtually the entire length of the province, the mountains are a source of both myth and legend, and play an important part in the history and culture of all its local peoples, most notably the Zulu. While it is in the foothills that much of the area's history has played out, the region's most significant claim to fame is the scenic splendour of its environs and the great diversity of its flora and fauna. The Drakensberg is perhaps the most striking example of South Africa's wide-ranging natural heritage, from the great diversity of its wildlife to the soaring heights of its undulating landscape. The semicircular façade of the **Amphitheatre** (ABOVE RIGHT) has become the most recognisable face of the entire range, and the **vulture restaurant hide at Giant's Castle** (OPPOSITE) is a remarkable place from which to view these creatures.

MPUMALANGA &
THE NORTH

Large parts of the northern reaches of South Africa – commonly thought of as dry bushveld – are in fact surprisingly green, the landscape dotted with colourful **cosmos** (ABOVE), and there are a number of rivers and waterfalls. Much of the generally rocky landscape of mountain and valley – as seen from the **Long Tom Pass** (OVERLEAF) – is covered either by lush grassland or vast stands of trees. Because of the extremes of landscape and vegetation, the northern areas are also a haven for adventurers, and on offer here are wilderness tours, day walks and overnight hikes, and some of the best birding in South Africa. This is also the home of the Kruger National Park, a vast rugged expanse of bushveld widely recognised as one of the finest wildlife sanctuaries in the world.

BLYDE RIVER CANYON & SURROUNDS

The historic little gold-mining town of **Pilgrim's Rest** (PREVIOUS PAGES) – where prospectors from as far afield as Australia headed in the days of the 'gold rush' in the 1870s – provides a gateway to the Escarpment and the rugged interior of hill and vale, river and stream. As the focal point of the **Blyde River Canyon Nature Reserve** (OPPOSITE), the region's dominant feature is the splendid **canyon** itself (ABOVE), a deep, intricately carved chasm that cuts deep down towards the Lowveld. It is one of the country's most recognisable natural features, and its rocky face of sandstone cliffs and the inclines that lead deep into the impressive **Blyde River Gorge** (OVERLEAF) mean that the canyon is the top drawcard to the area. The reserve itself is home to kudu, duiker, bushbuck and other antelope species, as well as primates (including vervet and samango monkeys) and a prolific birdlife that includes robins, shrikes, turacos (louries) and birds of prey such as lanner falcons, jackal buzzards and black eagles.

KRUGER NATIONAL PARK & PRIVATE RESERVES

The world-renowned Kruger National Park – stretching across the official border of Mpumalanga and Limpopo provinces – offers excellent game-viewing opportunities. Visitors are rewarded with frequent sightings of most of southern Africa's large mammals, among them **giraffe** (OPPOSITE) and **cheetah** (ABOVE LEFT), and herding mammals such as **plains zebra** (ABOVE RIGHT). Apart from mammals both large and small, Kruger is also blessed with a multitude of reptile, insect and bird species. It is largely for this reason – along with the diversity of its landscape and vegetation – that Kruger is one of the country's top tourist and wildlife destinations. Today, the national park is acclaimed across the globe, not only for its sound wildlife management and conservation programmes, but also for the quality of its visitors' facilities, especially accommodation, which varies from rustic bush camps to fully serviced bungalows and chalets. Adjoining the Kruger are several private reseves, including **Mala Mala** (OVERLEAF), Thornybush, Klaserie, Sabi Sands, Timbavati and Balule.

THE BIG FIVE

It is no secret that the Kruger National Park and the bushveld of which it forms the focus is southern Africa's most impressive wildlife showcase, and the primary destination for game-viewers, environmentalists and wildlife photographers. One of the main reasons for this is that it is home to all of Africa's Big Five: lion, elephant, leopard, rhino and buffalo. Once prolifically poached by trophy hunters, both the white and **black rhino** (ABOVE CENTRE) thrive in the northern bushveld, as do herds of **buffalo** (OPPOSITE). Visitors, however, still tend to home in on the country's big cats, and two important members are well established in the Kruger National Park: lion and leopard. King of the beasts is the **lion** (ABOVE LEFT), the largest of the continent's great cats. There are some 2 000 individuals in Kruger alone, and a pride of lion remains the top priority for many game-viewers armed with camera and notepad. Equally impressive, although considerably more elusive than their larger cousins, especially during the daylight hours, are **leopards** (ABOVE RIGHT), which are both powerful and graceful predators.

MAPANGUBWE & MUSINA

Although many of the settlements in the northern reaches of the country are small and may hardly be considered cosmopolitan in nature, it is the intimate surrounds and proud hospitality that continues to attract holidaymakers to such popular spots as the mineral springs of **Tshipise** (LEFT) on the outskirts of the Honnet Nature Reserve south-east of Musina (until fairly recently known as Messina). The little town of Musina itself is the country's northernmost settlement, virtually on the border between South Africa and Zimbabwe (OVERLEAF). The surrounding savanna, traditional home of the **Venda** (ABOVE RIGHT), is peppered with trees, ranging from acacia to karee, mopane to tamboti. Most significantly, however, the land is noted for its **baobab trees** (ABOVE LEFT), of which there are a number of spectacular specimens in the baobab reserve. To the west of Musina are the centuries-old ruins of Mapungubwe, a citadel settled by people of the Iron Age around a sandstone hill that has since yielded a remarkable array of archaeological finds, which have proved invaluable in learning more about these ancient peoples.

The Waterberg

Between the towns of Thabazimbi in the south and Lephalale (previously Ellisras) in the north lies the **Waterberg** (ABOVE), a biosphere reserve bordered by a series of mountain ranges. The wilderness area comprises an extensive **network of water sources** (OPPOSITE), and was established to protect the natural beauty of the immediate area and also the flora and fauna of the region. One of the most successful of these conservation efforts has been the rhino programme operating in and around the Lapalala Nature Reserve, which has helped stabilise and even increase the population of rhino, specifically the black rhino, as well as other rare or endangered species, including the sable and roan antelope. There are also thriving populations of white rhino, giraffe, Burchell's zebra, kudu, wildebeest and impala. Further south lie the Welgevonden Game Reserve and Marakele National Park, a conservation area that boasts an equally impressive list of wildlife, including leopard (which occur naturally here) and large mammals specifically introduced into the region in the 1990s, among them elephant, buffalo, hartebeest and hippo.

SUN CITY & LOST CITY

The landscape of the **Pilanesberg** (PREVIOUS PAGES) is one of shrubby bushveld covering the extinct crater of a volcano that is now eroded, giving way to a stark but beautiful backdrop to an area that is today prime game-viewing terrain. It is from this land of blue-skies and dusty veld that the spectacular Sun City complex arises. Entirely out of character with its arid, even desolate surrounds, this hotel and leisure facility is undoubtedly the country's most recognisable – its lavish architecture reminiscent of a long-forgotten kingdom originating in the mists of time. Its towering parapets stand out in vivid contrast to the blue of the sky, and the 'ancient' stonework of the **Bridge of Time** (LEFT) transports visitors to another realm entirely. One of the four hotels is the **Cascades Hotel** (ABOVE, LEFT and RIGHT), with its beach-style swimming pool, towering over the surrounding plains. **The Palace of the Lost City** (OVERLEAF), with its elaborate public rooms and lavish suites lit by dozens of chandeliers, glows warmly against the dark African night. Some two hours away, **Hartbeespoort Dam** (PAGES 124–125) is a popular getaway spot.

GAUTENG &
FREE STATE

The highveld that incorporates the provinces of Gauteng and the Free State has a climate that is probably as perfect as you can get anywhere: winter days may dawn with a layer of frost, but the daylight hours are crisp and bright, and the summer rains are refreshing rather than oppressive. What visitors will notice are the **mine dumps** (ABOVE), the origins of what is now South Africa's financial capital, Johannesburg, which developed from the simple camp that sprang up here after the discovery of gold in the late 1800s. Today, the City of Gold has developed into the country's most sophisticated city, and one that still plays a pivotal role in the economic development of the entire subcontinent.

City of Gold

Many people cannot understand why Johannesburg is not South Africa's capital city. While it may not have the scenic beauty of Cape Town or the political clout of Pretoria, it has everything else: a proud and distinct cultural and natural heritage, a thriving social profile – as testified by its many sports stadiums, for example, the **Wanderers Stadium** (ABOVE LEFT) – and a history built on prosperity and entrepreneurship. As such, Egoli – the City of Gold – has developed into a financial powerhouse, symbolised by the glittering **Diamond Building on Diagonal Street** (LEFT) in the heart of the city. It has, however, retained an unparalleled African identity, combining a cosmopolitan atmosphere with one that is distinctly traditional. Its modern skyline – from office blocks that scrape the sky to the imposing headgear so indicative of its pioneering **mining history** (OVERLEAF) – sits well with the market stalls and informal traders who sell indigenous arts and crafts on the busy pavements. It's no surprise, then, that even the massive cable-stayed **Nelson Mandela Bridge** (ABOVE RIGHT) is named after South Africa's most lauded statesman.

Nelson Mandela in hiding in a Colonel's flat before he was arrested in 1962 and brought to the Old Fort Prison Complex.

CONSTITUTION HILL

High on Braamfontein Ridge stands the Constitution Hill project, a tribute to those who fought in the struggle for democracy in South Africa. Today, the upgraded prison complex – including **Constitutional Court** (RIGHT) – has a polished look rich in the symbolism of a recovering nation: the original facebricks pave the Great Africa Steps and line the walls of the Court Chamber. The abundance of glass in the construction of the latter emphasises 'transparency', while the judges themselves – open to the full view of the visiting public – sit at the base of the amphitheatre-like space, in the dappled 'shade' of a wire tree, an example of the Afrocentric theme that pervades the entire structure. The **Old Fort** (ABOVE LEFT) encompasses Number Four, the cell-block reserved for black men, including Mohandas Gandhi, Robert Sobukwe and Albert Luthuli, but most notably Nelson Mandela, who was held in what is now commonly called the **Mandela Cell** (ABOVE RIGHT). The Fort also houses the old Women's Gaol, where Winnie Mandela and other prominent women were held during the struggle years.

GREATER JOHANNESBURG

Having risen from a landscape that was once the setting of the traditional homesteads of indigenous peoples and, in the late 1800s, the rows and rows of canvas tents that sheltered the prospectors who had streamed into the region to make their fortune from the gold that lay hidden in the rocky ground, metropolitan **Johannesburg** (ABOVE RIGHT) has a long and tumultuous history – one that is partly proud (it is the economic heart of the entire subcontinent) and partly shameful (the migrant labour that built it played a pivotal role in the segregation process that became the apartheid system). Today, however, the city of Johannesburg has shed its mantle of shame and oppression and, with such national icons as Constitution Hill, the **Gold Miners' Monument** (ABOVE LEFT), and the Apartheid Museum, is at the forefront of the reconciliation process. The latter-day city is a proud showcase of first-world South Africa: expansive shopping malls and entertainment arcades, fine eateries and world-class hotels, embodied in initiatives such as the **Melrose Arch** development (OPPOSITE).

Apartheid Museum

Like Constitution Hill, the **Apartheid Museum** (RIGHT) is one of the country's most impor-

tant monuments to the human suffering that emerged during the years of apartheid – 'the

system of segregation or discrimination on the grounds of race in force in South Africa

from 1948 to 1991'. The structure is sophisticated and impressive, the experience it offers

unlike any other similar project, evoking powerful images and emotions linked to the hor-

ror of that era. In a recreation of the sense of isolation suffered by so many South Africans

as a result of racist legislation, visitors are classified according to race and separated

from their companions as they are steered through exhibits that offer stark reminders of

the desolation fostered by the apartheid laws: the senseless executions, the brutality of

the security police – most often from the safety of their armoured **Casspirs** (ABOVE LEFT),

and the mass funerals and inhumane treatment of mineworkers in early Johannesburg,

depicted on one of the **museum's giant windows** (ABOVE RIGHT). The only consolation, at

the end, are the scenes of jubilation with the birth of democracy in the 1990s.

apartheid

/əˈpɑːtheɪt, əˈpɑːtheɪd/
n. the system of segregation or
discrimination on grounds of
race in force in South Africa
1948-91.

SOWETO

Beyond Johannesburg proper lies a world of contrasting colours and varied influences, offering an experience of a very different kind. Soweto, which was once a sadly neglected satellite of Greater Johannesburg to which thousands of black miners were banished when not underground, is one of South Africa's fastest growing cities. In the early years of its development, especially during the unforgiving apartheid era, SOuth WEstern TOwnship, impoverished and undeveloped (OPPOSITE), quickly earned a reputation for the lawlessness that pervaded its dusty streets. It was here that some of the struggle's most prominent leaders, including Nelson Mandela and Archbishop Emeritus Desmond Tutu, emerged to secure freedom for all of South Africa's oppressed. Following decades of a fierce determination for liberation and equality, the people of Soweto – also home to a number of high-profile personalities in arts, culture, politics and religion – have come forth triumphant, adopting a unique sense of entrepreneurship that has seen **informal trade** (ABOVE RIGHT) and the **taxi industry** (ABOVE LEFT) playing a vital role in the community.

The Cradle of Humankind

To the south-west of **Pretoria** (PREVIOUS PAGES) – a scenically splendid and leafy city that serves as the country's administrative capital – lies a series of underground caverns that has been hailed worldwide as the Cradle of Humankind. These caves were rediscovered at the end of the nineteenth century and, initially excavated largely for the deposits of bat guano, have since yielded a priceless treasure of archaeological finds that has earned the region status as a World Heritage Site. It is within these **dripstone caves** (ABOVE LEFT) that archaeologists from the Transvaal Museum and the University of the Witwatersrand – most notably Dr Robert Broom, after whom the latter-day museum is named – unearthed a number of fossils, including hominid remains. The most significant of these excavations was the discovery, in 1947, of the two-million-year-old cranium of what came to be known as 'Mrs Ples' (*Plesianthropus transvaalensis*) in the **Sterkfontein Caves** (RIGHT). Another important site is that of **Kromdraai** (ABOVE RIGHT), a disused mineshaft that yielded several fragments of a skull which, assembled by Broom, came to be known as 'Kromdraai Man'.

THE MAGALIESBERG

To the west of Pretoria is a stretch of low-lying hills that extends some 120 kilometres towards the town of Rustenburg. These picturesque hills, surprisingly green and fruitful – quite literally, as this is an important citrus and subtropical fruit-farming area – remain popular as a holiday destination and weekend getaway. Rising no more than 300 metres, they are interlaced with hiking trails and walks, and seen from the air – **hot-air ballooning** (LEFT) is a popular drawcard – they offer endless vistas of the Magaliesberg Nature Reserve. The wildlife to be found here includes the elusive leopard and the brown hyena, and it is also prime birding terrain, the most significant species being the Cape vulture. Here too is the popular **Magalies Meander** art route (ABOVE LEFT) and another favourite leisure spot, particularly for locals, is the **Hartbeespoort Dam** (ABOVE RIGHT), with the sought-after residential area of **Kosmos** on its shores. The reservoir itself, which is fed by the waters of both the Crocodile and Magalies rivers, is vital to the irrigation of land in the area. The **Gariep Dam** (OVERLEAF), to the south in the Free State, is also a popular resort.

GOLDEN GATE HIGHLANDS NATIONAL PARK

The Free State is an exceptionally beautiful province, its relatively flat landscapes – from its extensive farmlands to its vast wilderness areas – bathed in swathes of earth tones. These range from the bright yellows of the **poplar trees** (PREVIOUS PAGES) that have come to epitomise the Free State countryside to the golden hues of the sheer cliff faces that encircle the **Golden Gate Highlands National Park** (OPPOSITE and ABOVE RIGHT), the province's premier nature reserve. Set in the valley of the Little Caledon River, the park is most noted for the grand scale of the towering sandstone peaks and ridges that back onto the ramparts of the Lesotho highlands to the south. Although the Mountain Kingdom, Lesotho, itself is very different in both nature and make-up, its looming massifs and hilly plains are a veritable adventure playground for hikers, mountain climbers and pony trekkers, the latter taking their cue from the experienced **Basotho horsemen** (ABOVE LEFT) who traverse the countryside on the ubiquitous Basotho ponies, which are still the largely rural population's chief mode of transport.

CLARENS & SURROUNDS

Crowned by the Golden Gate Highlands National Park to the east, the 'golden triangle' created by the Free State towns of Fouriesburg, Clarens and Bethlehem is indeed that – a geometric section of land characterised by wheat fields, **sunflowers** (ABOVE) and maize, ideal for a picturesque **train trip** (LEFT). Much of the area is now known as the Riemland, a name that originated in the days when game was plentiful and early settlers hunted the animals for both their meat and their hide, which served as a means of barter. Today, this is largely farmland, much of it given over to crops and cattle. In recent years, the charming little town of Clarens is best known for the Artists' Amble, a fascinating craft route that takes in the galleries and studios of local artists, as well as for the ancient Bushman paintings that adorn the rock faces of the sandstone hills in the vicinity of Fouriesburg (OVERLEAF) and Clarens to the south-west.

GREAT KAROO
& INTERIOR

The vast arid interior, incorporating large parts of the Northern Cape, is characterised by occasional dolerite hills, ridges and outcrops, as well as flat-topped hills known as mesas, notably in the aptly-named **Valley of Desolation** near Graaff-Reinet (ABOVE). The sand here is dry, the episodic rivers for the most part waterless, lined only with stark thorn trees and small scrubby stands of thick-leaved vegetation. Although the land is unsuited to any sort of agricultural usage, the hard, cracked ground makes for good sheep country and, in parts, good horse-rearing territory. The Great Karoo, however, and the north-western interior is a land of almost surreal beauty, one endowed with an eerie tranquillity and a peace that can only come with the emptiness that seems to ring in your ears.

THE GREAT KAROO

The stark beauty of the Great Karoo comes at a great price: water. The broader region receives no more than about 250 millimetres annually – and, more often than not, considerably less – and the result is that every attempt is made not only to conserve this all-important resource, but also to extract it from every possible source. The farmers resort to **windmill pumps** and innumerable dams (OPPOSITE) in order to sustain the land. Farming here is challenging to say the least (ABOVE RIGHT), with vast, open and empty stretches unable to sustain even the hardiest of crops. But the resoluteness of the people is also inspiring and, dotted across these plains are small villages and rural communities, isolated pockets of an indigenous culture that has seen little change over the centuries. One memorable stop is the little town of Nieu-Bethesda, best known for the curiosity that has come to be known as **The Owl House** (ABOVE LEFT), the home of and monument to the eccentric Miss Helen Martins, who, with her assistant, crafted the cement and glass menagerie that peoples her property.

THE GREAT INTERIOR

The interior of the Northern Cape is dominated by one large city and its 'Great Hole': Kimberley is the commercial, administrative and industrial focus of the entire hinterland and makes for a fascinating diversion in what is otherwise a rather **featureless landscape** (LEFT). It is not a big city, even by South African standards, but it has come a long way since the days when it consisted of little more than a conglomeration of tents, shacks and a series of dry paths carved into the dust by the wagon wheels of fortune-seekers heading for the promise of wealth that lay in the diamond fields. In its heyday, Kimberley was a thriving place, one of untold riches, boundless opportunity and keen entrepreneurship, and today it may be considerably more restful than when it was populated almost exclusively by miners and missionaries. Today the tributes to these great founding fathers may be seen at the **homestead museum of missionary Robert Moffat** (ABOVE LEFT) in Kuruman and the **Diamond Workers' Monument** (ABOVE RIGHT) at the Kimberley Civic Centre.

KGALAGADI & THE NORTH

Tucked away in the far northern corner of the country lies one of the subcontinent's most remarkable conservation feats: the **Kgalagadi Transfrontier Park** (PREVIOUS PAGES) between South Africa and Botswana is Africa's pioneer trans-national reserve and one that has set the standard for many other such reserves on the continent. The region – arid and apparently inhospitable, but bathed in a deep glow of red, yellow and burnt orange – boasts a surprising diversity of floral and faunal life. Although best known for its blazing red sand dunes, the majestic oryx (gemsbok) and the tsamma melon (wild watermelon) – all-important in this thirsty landscape – the semidesert landscape of the Kalahari is also home to other large antelope, such as the **blue wildebeest** (ABOVE LEFT), as well as smaller species, including the ubiquitous **springbok** (OPPOSITE). And simply because it is such a haven for so many herbivorous mammals, it also has its fair share of predators – most notably the **black-maned lion** (ABOVE CENTRE), the **bateleur eagle and the jackal** (ABOVE RIGHT).

THE KALAHARI & AUGRABIES FALLS

The region commonly known as the Kalahari – strictly a semidesert wilderness as opposed to a true desert – is the traditional home of the **Bushman people** (PREVIOUS PAGES) and a place not immediately associated with an abundance of either flora or fauna. Nothing, however, can be further from the truth. It is, in fact, home to both the **oryx, or gemsbok, and the lion** (RIGHT), a number of even more prolific antelope species and even big game species such as cheetah, leopard, wild dog and hyena. This is a land best known for its flat grasslands, distant horizon and endless sky, and although the landscape is dotted here and there with acacia trees, the vegetation is generally stark (ABOVE). However, in the middle of what seems a godforsaken portion of Africa, one of southern Africa's most significant natural features breaks the monotony of the world that surrounds it. It is here that the impressive **Augrabies Falls** (OVERLEAF) interrupts the powerful flow of the mighty Orange River as it winds its way to the Atlantic Ocean on the west coast.

THE RICHTERSVELD

The Richtersveld is at its most impressive when the sun begins to set over the rocky ridges that skirt the ruggedly beautiful but mercilessly inhospitable veld of the area. This often desperately dry wilderness that forms the border between the Northern Cape province and Namibia, with its harsh sun, is mostly empty of human habitation and the small villages that dot the banks of the **Orange River** (LEFT and ABOVE RIGHT) are pitifully few and far between, separated by an endless stretch of sand scattered with rocky outcrops and the looming silhouettes of lone stands of **quiver trees** (ABOVE LEFT).

The **Richtersveld National Park** (OVERLEAF), to the north of Springbok, the tiny 'capital' of this broad region, consists mostly of far-reaching plains that feature little more than a smattering of boulders embraced by distant mountains. The park itself is a formidable wilderness, the only sign of human life being the remnants of trails scratched from the dry earth by long-gone colonial pioneers as they made their way, baking under the glare of the Richtersveld sun, to the diamond fields to the north.

THE CEDERBERG

Where the semidesert of the Karoo merges with the coastal plains of the West Coast lie the open veld and rugged mountainscapes of the Cederberg, a series of rocky crags and stone faces sculpted over the centuries by sand and wind. The rock formations include the much-photographed Maltese Cross, the Wolfberg Cracks and the **Wolfberg Arch** (ABOVE) but the corrosive nature of the elements here mean that there are also a number of natural caves (OPPOSITE), many of which are decorated with the rock paintings of their early Bushman inhabitants. The Stadsaal Caves and Elephant Cave may be the most famous, but there are also some fine examples of rock art along the Sevilla Trail near Clanwilliam, where the rare Clanwilliam cedar trees characterise the valley slopes.

In the Little Karoo to the east, lies the **Anysberg Nature Reserve** (OVERLEAF), created to preserve the natural flora of the area and to reintroduce the game originally found in the region. From the Cederberg, a four-hour drive south along the Cape West Coast ends with those famous views of **Table Bay and Table Mountain** (PAGES 180–181).

First published in 2005 by Struik Publishers (a division of New Holland Publishing (South Africa) (Pty) Ltd)

New Holland Publishing is a member of Johnnic Communications Ltd

Garfield House, 86–88 Edgware Road, London W2 2EA, United Kingdom
www.newhollandpublishers.com

80 McKenzie Street, Cape Town 8001, South Africa
www.struik.co.za

14 Aquatic Drive, Frenchs Forest, NSW 2086, Australia

218 Lake Road, Northcote, Auckland, New Zealand

ISBN 1 77007 145 8

1 3 5 7 9 10 8 6 4 2

Publishing Manager: Dominique le Roux
Managing Editor: Lesley Hay-Whitton
Designers: Sian Marshall and Martin Jones
Editor: Christine Grant
Proofreader: Helen de Villiers
Indexer: Ethné Clarke
Reproduction by Hirt & Carter Cape (Pty) Ltd
Printed and bound by Craft Print International Ltd

Log on to our photographic website www.imagesofafrica.co.za for an African experience.

Picture Credits

AB — Andrew Bannister
AM — Apartheid Museum
CLB — Colour Library
ET — Erhardt Thiel
FM — Fiona McIntosh
FvH — Friederich von Hörsten
GD — Gerhard Dreyer
HvH — Hein von Hörsten
IOA — Images of Africa

JdP — Jéan du Plessis
JH — John Hodgekiss
JM — Jacqui Murray
JR — John Robinson
KY — Keith Young
LvH — Lanz von Hörsten
OM — Owen Middleton
P&BP — Peter & Beverly Pickford
RdH — Roger de la Harpe

RH — Rod Haestier
RO — Raymond Oberholzer
RvJ — Rhone van Jaarsveld
SA — Shaen Adey
SAL — South African Library
SI — Sun International
VB — Vanessa Burger
WK — Walter Knirr

Pg 1	HvH/IOA	Pg 44 (b)	RO/IOA	Pg 81 (a)	RdH/IOA	Pg 116	WK/IOA	Pg 158	RO/IOA
Pg 2–3	LvH/IOA	Pg 45	FvH/IOA	Pg 81 (b)	JR/IOA	Pg 117	FvH/IOA	Pg 159 (a)	JdP/IOA
Pg 4–5	HvH/IOA	Pg 46	LvH/IOA	Pg 82	VB/IOA	Pg 118–119	WK/IOA	Pg 159 (b)	RO/IOA
Pg 8–9	HvH/IOA	Pg 47 (a)	HvH/IOA	Pg 83 (a)	VB/IOA	Pg 120–123	All SI	Pg 160	RO/IOA
Pg 10–11	JdP/IOA	Pg 47 (b)	JdP/IOA	Pg 83 (b)	SA/IOA	Pg 124–125	HvH/IOA	Pg 161 (a)	WK/IOA
Pg 12–13	HvH/IOA	pg 48–49	RH/IOA	Pg 83 (c)	SA/IOA	Pg 126–127	WK/IOA	Pg 161 (b)	CLB/IOA
Pg 14–15	JdP/IOA	Pg 50 (a)	JdP/IOA	Pg 84	RdH/IOA	Pg 128	WK/IOA	Pg 162–163	JdP/IOA
Pg 16–17	SA/IOA	Pg 50 (b)	HvH/IOA	Pg 85	FM/IOA	Pg 129 (a)	WK/IOA	Pg 164 (a)	JdP/IOA
Pg 18	JdP/IOA	Pg 50 (c)	LvH/IOA	Pg 86	SA/IOA	Pg 129 (b)	RvJ/IOA	Pg 164 (b)	VB/IOA
Pg 19	JdP/IOA	Pg 51	HvH/IOA	Pg 87	VB/IOA	Pg 130–131	HvH/IOA	Pg 164 (c)	JdP/IOA
Pg 20 (a)	LvH/IOA	pg 52	JdP/IOA	Pg 88	VB/IOA	Pg 132 (a)	JH	Pg 165	HvH/IOA
Pg 20 (b)	SA/IOA	Pg 53 (a)	JdP/IOA	Pg 89	LvH/IOA	Pg 132 (b)	JH	Pg 166–167	FvH/IOA
Pg 21	FvH/IOA	Pg 53 (b)	JdP/IOA	Pg 90–91	WK/IOA	Pg 133	JH	Pg 168	HvH/IOA
Pg 22–23	HvH/IOA	Pg 54–55	JdP/IOA	Pg 92	SA/IOA	Pg 134	RvJ/IOA	Pg 169	VB/IOA
Pg 24 (a)	JdP/IOA	Pg 56 (a)	LvH/IOA	Pg 93 (a)	SA/IOA	Pg 135 (a)	WK/IOA	Pg 170–171	FvH/IOA
Pg 24 (b)	FvH/IOA	Pg 56 (b)	HvH/IOA	Pg 93 (b)	WK/IOA	Pg 135 (b)	RO/IOA	Pg 172	JdP/IOA
Pg 24 (c)	SA/IOA	Pg 57	HvH/IOA	Pg 94–95	LHV	Pg 136–137	All AM	Pg 173 (a)	JdP/IOA
Pg 25	SA/IOA	Pg 58–59	HvH/IOA	Pg 96–97	KY/IOA	Pg 138 (a)	SA/IOA	Pg 173 (b)	WK/IOA
Pg 26 (a)	HvH/IOA	Pg 60	SA/IOA	Pg 98–99	FvH/IOA	Pg 138 (b)	SA/IOA	Pg 174–175	JdP/IOA
Pg 26 (b)	HvH/IOA	Pg 61	LvH/IOA	Pg 100–101	FvH/IOA	Pg 139	SA/IOA	Pg 176	OM/IOA
Pg 26 (c)	ET/IOA	Pg 62–63	SA/IOA	Pg 102	FvH/IOA	Pg 140–141	JM/IOA	Pg 177	HvH/IOA
Pg 27	FvH/IOA	Pg 64	GD/IOA	Pg 103 (a)	FvH/IOA	Pg 142 (a)	SA/IOA	Pg 178–179	JdP/IOA
Pg 28–29	FvH/IOA	Pg 65	LvH/IOA	Pg 103 (b)	LvH/IOA	Pg 142 (b)	SA/IOA	Pg 180–181	OM/IOA
Pg 30	SA/IOA	Pg 66–67	HvH/IOA	Pg 104–105	WK/IOA	Pg 143	WK/IOA	Pg 184–185	HvH/IOA
Pg 31	SA/IOA	Pg 68–69	LvH/IOA	Pg 106 (a)	FvH/IOA	Pg 144	WK/IOA		
Pg 32	SA/IOA	Pg 70–71	HvH/IOA	Pg 106 (b)	FvH/IOA	Pg 145 (a)	SA/IOA		
Pg 33	LvH/IOA	Pg 72	FvH/IOA	Pg 107	JdP/IOA	Pg 145 (b)	HvH/IOA		
Pg 34–35	LvH/IOA	Pg 73 (a)	JdP/IOA	Pg 108–109	LvH/IOA	Pg 146–147	FvH/IOA		
Pg 36	ET/IOA	Pg 73 (b)	FvH/IOA	Pg 110 (a)	AB/IOA	Pg 148–149	HvH/IOA		
Pg 37	SA/IOA	Pg 73 (c)	FvH/IOA	Pg 110 (b)	AB/IOA	Pg 150	HvH/IOA		
Pg 38	SA/IOA	Pg 74–75	SAL	Pg 110 (c)	P&BP/IOA	Pg 151 (a)	HvH/IOA		
Pg 39	HvH/IOA	Pg 76	FvH/IOA	Pg 111	LvH/IOA	Pg 151 (b)	WK/IOA		
Pg 40–41	HvH/IOA	Pg 77 (a)	SA/IOA	Pg 112	WK/IOA	Pg 152	WK/IOA		
Pg 42	FvH/IOA	Pg 77 (b)	KY/IOA	Pg 113 (a)	WK/IOA	Pg 153	HvH/IOA		
Pg 43	FvH/IOA	Pg 78–79	KY/IOA	Pg 113 (b)	HvH/IOA	Pg 154–155	WK/IOA		
Pg 44 (a)	HvH/IOA	Pg 80	WK/IOA	Pg 114–115	FvH/IOA	Pg 156–157	JdP/IOA		

Index